LAB MONKEY:
I SURVIVED
REVISED

A True Story

MICHAEL YOUNG

authorHOUSE®

AuthorHouse™
1663 Liberty Drive
Bloomington, IN 47403
www.authorhouse.com
Phone: 1 (800) 839-8640

Published by AuthorHouse 08/17/2018

ISBN: 978-1-5462-5642-7 (sc)
ISBN: 978-1-5462-5641-0 (e)

Acknowledgements

To author Antoinette Tunique Smith: Thank you for helping me open up and share my past. (**www.straighttothepointbooks.com**)

To my co-associate Malory Rogers: Thank you.

To my brothers, sisters, and children: May God look after you.

Special thanks and rest in peace Isaac Hayes: Thanks for looking out for my favorite uncle.

And a special shout out to Bobby O Jay Program Director of AM 1070 WDIA, Memphis, TN The First Black Run Radio Station in the U.S.

To Mom...

I miss you very much...

Chapter 1: The Beginning

It was a warm summer night in 1954. I remember my mother saying grandma called home to tell one of her brothers to meet her halfway in the park on her way home from work. He never made it to the park, or either he was too slow. My mom never could remember what delayed him, but he had wished a many days that he would have left as soon as she called. Maybe she would still be alive today…or maybe not.

She was stabbed three times by her ex-boyfriend. My mom said she always knew he would kill her one day, but she thought it would be from the multiple beatings he gave her every weekend. It seems as if every time he got drunk, he'd find another reason to beat her over and over again. She and her brothers swore one day they would kill him.

My grandmother left behind four sons and one daughter, Carol, my mother. They were split up. My mom was sent one place and the boys were sent to four different places. Back then, you went wherever someone would feed you. It didn't matter if they were kin or not. Sadly, they never saw each other again, which started what I call a generational curse.

I was born in April of 1959. My mother had just turned 18. I was the fifth of five children. My mother had a child just about every year. I was considered special because I was the only surviving son. My mother had her first son, my older brother, when she was fourteen. He died when he was 2 months old – from pneumonia they said. After that, she only had her three daughters and me to take care of, and I required a lot of care. I was born **blind with a severe case** of cataracts. My mother said I stayed in the hospital for months **before** the doctors would let me come home. As I got older, the cataracts got worse.

I could remember as early as age three, people asking my mom "who is his dad?" My mother either didn't know or she just didn't want to tell because she would always change the subject by saying "God is his daddy, now let it be."

I was born with light brown eyes and blue circles around my pupils. They were crossed very bad and my skin was a pale olive color. In those days, the insurance men were white and they would come to your house and pick up your payment. If you didn't have the money, he would get his payment another way. I don't have to spell it out. You know what I mean.

My mother, struggling with four children without fathers, thought it would be a better life for them if she gave away my sisters to friends and relatives. She was still very depressed about the death of my older brother. She still grieved. She was always crying because she felt it was her fault. My two older sisters were mixed and my baby sister was pure African American. Of course, she was the hardest one to find a place for. No one wanted "a black ugly child." I was four years old and I remember I had no one but my mom, all my sisters were gone.

I remember I was about 4 years old and my mother got involved with a man who she claimed was a hard worker. It turned out that he was just like the others, abusing and always stayed gone in the streets running around with other women. My mom had four more children from him and he never let me forget I was his stepchild as he would so rudely say it. I was still in and out of the hospital. I was always afraid that my mother would leave me forever because I knew her husband would be so happy if I never returned. I would stay in the hospital one to two months at a time. The cataracts kept coming back and my vision was getting worse. By the time I turned six, I had had 11 major surgeries. I can remember on a Monday, my mother would tell me it was time for me to go back in the hospital for a while. I hated to go back to that hospital because I knew there was always a chance that I may never come home.

As much as I hated going in the hospital, I hated staying at home with my other siblings and a new stepfather who treated me like shit. I never understood why my mom would have more kids when she gave some of her first set away. I had four brothers and one sister, no I didn't miscount. There was one brother born right after me, I will explain later. Three boys and a daughter were my abusive stepfather's kids.

Where did I fit in in this family? Nowhere is exactly how felt. I remember one Christmas like it was yesterday. My brothers all got pop-guns and cowboy hats - the ones with the stars on them. I asked my mother what did I get and my stepdad yelled "nothing! We didn't know you would be here, you being in and out of the hospital." I remember thinking wow, why was my mom letting this man treat me this way. So, as the other kids played with their toys, I slowly walked into another room and cried myself to sleep. My mom later came and got me for dinner, and while I noticed one of my brothers was still eating, I played with his pop-guns. My stepdad saw me and grabbed me and shouted never to play with his sons toys again because if I broke them he would break my ass. My mom just looked at me helpless. She didn't say a word.

Every time my stepfather was around, he would tell me to stay away from him and his sons. I guess this was about the time I became a television nerd. I knew everything that came on and every commercial.

My brothers would laugh and pick at me because I had to sit so close to see, but I didn't care. This was my world. The TV allowed me to escape to another place, be another person, and live another life.

Chapter 2: Stepchild

I was just starting kindergarten. I enjoyed going to school. I got to meet different people, some nicer and some not so nice, but anything beat being at home and in the hospital. My mother was waiting on me one day when I came home from school. She said it was time I go back to the hospital for another eye exam. I hated to hear this because I was in school and enjoyed learning different things. I was also catching on to the fact that they were doing more than just plain eye exams. An eye exam does not require you to stay in the hospital. I would stay in the hospital for two to four weeks for supposedly an eye exam.

I was always greeted when I came to the hospital by lots of doctors and nurses discussing my condition, whispering and going over my chart. You would think I had the plague. After they would admit me into a room they give me fluid. I can't remember exactly the taste, but I remember it was green and pink. They would then take a urine and stool sample. They would insert needles into my arms and legs and strap me to the bed. The doctor would tell me to count backwards from 100, and by the time I reached 95, I was asleep. When I finally did wake up, I would have all type of alarms on my chest. If I tried to move, they would go off and nurses would run in monitoring the equipment and changing fluid in bags. This went on repeatedly throughout the night. Just like clockwork, they would run in and document - like a science experiment or something.

Three to four days would pass. They would feed me well with three full course meals a day with ice cream and fruit for snacks and dessert. For three days straight, they would take blood samples, skin tests and finally an eye test. There were several different doctors - older ones and younger ones. There was this one doctor that I remember that must have been at my birth because was always there. He was constantly monitoring, record keeping and examining. He had to be very important because when his name was mentioned, everybody listened. I often wondered if he was Doctor Frankenstein.

Chapter 3: Back and Forth

When you are in the hospital for a long period of time, it starts to get to you mentally. I liked staying in the hospital rather than being at home though. I guess you can say it was the better of my two evils. The nurses were very nice and I liked getting three square meals a day and the snacks.

"Good morning Michael" said one of the nurses, "I guess you're pretty excited you will be going home tomorrow."

I could hear the other nurse whisper to her "he will be back." I was not going to focus on that. I was just too excited to be going home. I could never sleep the night before. It was always hard for me to recover after they took off the bandages, the IVs and unstrapped me. They made it look as if nothing else had been done to me besides the supposed eye exam. There was this one place they had an IV that always hurt more than the other. Everyone would always ask "how are you feeling?, Do you feel nauseated or weak?" I would feel all of that, but I didn't let them know because I was ready to go home, so I would just say I feel fine.

My mother would finally arrive, and she would smile and give me hugs and kisses as if I was her only child. She would tell me how much everyone missed me and how glad she will be to have me home. "How do you feel," she also asked, but it was hard for me to speak after I was released. I don't know why. So I would just shake my head ok. She talked to the doctors and they told her I would need to come back soon for another recheck for my eyes. Now I'm not a baby anymore and I know they did more to me than just check my eyes. They did look at my eyes, but it wasn't that often. I always wondered why they were doing other things to me. I was getting older now, and lots of things were beginning to make sense, but, for some reason, I never told my mom.

While driving home, all I could think about was mom's home cooked meals. The hospital food wasn't bad, but it sure couldn't beat my moms. My mom asked about another boy across the street that was in the hospital. She asked if I saw him much? I told her yes he was in the hospital almost every time I was in there. I also told her about the little girl that lived in our neighborhood. She was in the hospital as well, but she looked very sad all the time and very sick. My mother looked at me with a strange look on her face. She seemed surprised.

We finally made it home. Mom said, "go unpack", and get ready for supper. I noticed mom ran straight to the phone. What was on her mind or what did I say that made her so upset. I unpacked and went outside to play where everyone else was. Mom was still on the phone. It was such a pretty day outside. It seemed like the whole neighborhood was out. I heard someone from a far yell "hey Michael, look everyone its Mike. One of the boys said "man you been in the hospital a long time." You look ok but your eyes are crossed up. (everyone laughing) This really hurt me but I couldn't let them see me cry so I would just ease back into the house and go into my world where I was in-charge: the television - my world away from home.

My mother eventually got off the phone. She smiled and came over to talk to me. "Michael", she would say, how was your stay in the hospital? Do you remember what they did to you? I told her it was ok. Some of the people were nice and all I can remember is them putting a lot of drops in my eyes and shinning bright lights in my face. She asked how well could I see? I told her I can see the TV a little better than before. She said the doctor took something from the back of my eyes that was suppose to help me see better and that they set me up another appointment to come back next month. That was the last thing I wanted, but I guess my mom knew what they were doing, at least I thought she did. I sure hope the little boy across the street is ok, my mom said. "I hear he is still in the hospital. "Lord have mercy." as she walked away mumbling under her breath.

My eyesight began to get worse. I was tripping and falling over stuff. I realized I could no longer judge distance. I didn't know near from far anymore. It got so bad that they increased my bifocals in my glasses. I looked like I was Chinese. My eyes were so small in those glasses. They were so thick that people would stop and stare at me. The adults felt sorry, but the kids would laugh and point. There was so much medicine in the glasses that they looked like magnifying glass. When the light in the house or the sunlight hit my eyes, it caused more damage. I knew it was just a matter of time before I would be back in the hospital having another unwanted surgery.

Chapter 4: Going Home Again

Time passed and it was getting harder and harder to deal with the bifocals. I think the hardest thing was family members and some kids in the neighborhood always making fun of me. I could feel the time nearing for me to go back in the hospital. It made me sad to think about it, but I knew I had no choice. My mother would have a family gathering as a way to cheer me up every time I got ready to go back into the hospital. I guess they never really knew if I would return home. My uncle always showed up. I had four uncles, and he was ok, but he made fun of me whenever he got drunk. He didn't visit that much, but he knew I was always in and out of the hospital. He was the one that started calling me "lab monkey." "Oh there he is," he would say, "my nephew, the lab monkey, cross eyed, thick glasses, can't talk, blue eyed monkey." He would say all this stuff in front of the other kids and mom. Everyone would laugh except my mom and my other uncles would see my mother getting angry and ask him to stop. An argument would always break out and spoil the party. I clearly remember my uncle saying to my mom, "you know that boy is not normal sis. He has bad eyes, you don't know who his real father is, and he is always in and out of the hospital, and they ought to keep his dam lil ugly ass for something."

That was it. My mother had enough, she yelled, "you wrong old man and get yo drunk ass out my house now." My uncle left, but as he walked on the front porch and slammed the door he yelled back. "Sis you know something is going on at that hospital. Don't be no fool!" Next thing I heard was his car door slam. While I was upstairs, I could hear everybody's voices. There was a lot of murmuring and talking really low. Earlier, it had been so loud, and there had been so much laughter. One by one, everyone started to leave.

A few relatives stayed around playing cards and loud music, laughing and talking. This was the last time I saw my mom and her brothers together. I had one uncle that was my favorite. His name was Thomas. He came around to check on my mom every now and then. He used to talk to me and try and encourage me. He would give me advice and he told me I would grow out of my condition. He used to be a manager for this famous R&B singer. He would bring me over old clothes that the singer would throw out. They were a little big, but when I found out they were from a famous person, I didn't care. I felt so special. He died a couple of years later and that famous R&B singer paid for his funeral. When I saw Issac Hayes at the funeral, I nearly passed out. Wow, I couldn't wait to get home and tell everyone in the neighborhood *I, Michael Young, wore Issac Hayes' clothes.*

Chapter 5: Uncle

A Long time passed before we stopped talking about my uncle. My evil stepfather had left my mother for some other woman. He said he was just tired of her poor black ass running back and forth to the hospital with my retarded ass. I was so happy he left, even though it hurt mom very bad.

The next day, the hospital called and said they wanted to set up an appointment for my mother to bring me back for another eye surgery. My mother called me over to her and said, "look Michael, you need to be brave now, cause these doctors are going to help you. They said they gonna remove your lens or something so your eyes can get better." Yea, I thought to myself, another experiment. I want my eyes to get better, but what else is gonna happen to me there. Two weeks passed and mom was taking me back to the hospital. It was the same scenario - the greetings and the fake smiles, some were real, but I often wondered what was behind those smiles, what were their real motives. This time was different. There were old doctors and young doctors and some familiar faces. Why did I need so many doctors? One doctor that I remembered from last time said "hi Michael, how are you? I promise we will take better care of you and you will see so much better when you leave."

They checked me in the same as before, but on the way to the lab, I saw the same little girl I had seen before. She was in the waiting area. I waved at her, but she did not wave back. She looked very scared.

Mom walked up and asked if I was ok. I said that I was a little scared. She said "Everything will be ok, The doctor said they would take good care of you. I believe the surgery will go well and they will put you in this room for monitoring." I started to walk towards the room where mom pointed they will keep me for monitoring, and a man quickly walked up and closed the curtains.

Finally, I was in my room. Mom said the little boy in our neighborhood was here and I also told her about the little girl from last time whom we did not know. It was very strange they would be getting admitted the same time as myself, and they did not have eye problems.

Mom kissed me on the forehead and said "I have to go now baby, love ya. see you soon."

"Bye mom," I replied.

"bye sweetheart," and she walked out the door.

I was really feeling bad because my surgery was in the morning, and by now, I was very tired.

I had just about dozed off when the nurses started coming in drawing blood, taking my vitals and hooked up the IV. The procedure was the same. They gave me a pill and 9 cups of green liquid to drink. They took a urine and stool sample. Several of the doctors begin to come in. One asked how did I feel as he looked into my eyes with a bright light. He examined my eyes a very long time as another doctor stood back and watched.

This was a little unusual. They checked my heart rate, then they filled about three vials of blood. They gave me some more pills and the room was in a dead silence. The doctors were still standing there, maybe four or five of them. There was this one doctor who stared at me strangely. He didn't take his eyes off of me, but yet, he did not say a word as the other doctors were whispering among each other. I never saw him before or did I see when he entered the room, but he gave me a peace, and I fell deeply asleep.

Chapter 6: Going Back

It appears that I was dreaming. I kept hearing muffled voices and seeing all these lights and silhouettes of people through the lights. I can feel hands touching all over my body, poking and sticking me with objects. I didn't know if I was dreaming or if this was real. Suddenly, I became sleepy and I could feel something cold going through my veins, then I was asleep.

I don't know how long I was asleep, but I finally woke up. I couldn't see because there were pads all over my eyes. My arms, legs, chest and feet were strapped down. I had needles in both my arms and one of my legs. I was screaming and hollering. The nurses were scared as they ran into the room. They didn't know how long I had been awake. I can hear the nurses talking to each other. They didn't know what to do, "calm him down," said one of the ladies. I was in so much pain. I felt helpless because I was tied down like a rabid animal. A man walked into the room and yelled, "Put him back to sleep! Dammit, he should not be awake yet." I saw a shadow coming towards my face with the mask and I knew once I smelled that gas I would soon be back to sleep.

I don't know how long I was out, but when I finally woke up, I heard a man's voice, "Hi Michael, how do you feel?" I didn't know how to answer that because I had pads still over my eyes. I still had needles in my legs and chest. My chest hurt because every time I move, the needles stick me deeper. I was still strapped down and could not move. My mouth was very dry and I could not speak. The doctor told me to hold up one finger for yes, and two for no. He told me my mother was here for the operation and that she stayed a while, but she left. "The operation was a success," he said, "but we had to do some more to make sure your body wont reject any of the medication you will be given when you are released. Are you in any pain Michael?" I held up one finger as he earlier instructed me to do.

"Ok," he said, "I will get you something to make you feel a little better. I know you are a little uncomfortable, but we had to strap you down and put the IVs in in order to perform all the necessary tests that were needed in order for your surgery to be a success."

I was hooked up to a monitor. I had needles stuck in my legs and chest and he had the nerve to ask me if I was in pain. He said I can't have any solid foods for another 24 hours. They had to do more test and they wanted me to drink more of the green fluid. They gave me so much fluid to drink that I lost count. I was constantly in pain and it took them forever to give me something.

Lots of time had passed by and mom still had not come back to see me. The only people I saw were nurses and doctors coming in and out of my room. Most of the time, I was asleep because they had me so sedated. One nurse came in and said "good news Michael, we are going to try and change the pads on the eyes to see how much you have improved."

I can feel the cool air hitting my face. I was still tied to the bed and I had just about gotten used to the needles all over my body. I can't help but think why are they lying to me? What can they want from a poor little black boy. I know it's more to it then eye surgery. Another nurse entered. She was checking the monitor and changing the pads again on my eyes. They would also swab my mouth because my lips were so dry and brittle. Another nurse came in later and put cream all over my skin which made me feel a little warm.

A week later I was moved to another floor. While I was on this floor, I noted there were other children - all black. There was a total of eight of them; two of them were girls. One was the little girl that I had seen before when I was admitted. Some of them were still moaning. All of the kids were wrapped up in a thin blanket like me. There were guys in suits, some nurses and lots of doctors. The nurses would come over and bring us some pills and more of the green chalky fluid. I noticed we all had bugs flying all around us. We were all sitting in a room like we were pigs being fed in a pig stein. *What was going on here?* I thought. We were treated like a bunch of freaks.

Finally, the nurses had given everyone their medicine and everyone was nearly sleep except for a few that were still moaning. I don't know how long we were asleep, but when I woke up, I was in another room alone. My body felt so numb. I could not feel anything. It seemed like my entire body was paralyzed. They had taken out all the needles and had placed pads all over my body where the needles were except for one arm, it still had an IV in it.

Every day they would take more tests, draw more blood and test more excretions. I remember I woke up scared and angry. I was scared because I didn't know what the hell was going on, and angry that I may not make it out of here alive. Later, the numbness was wearing off. My hands were still tied to the bed. I could feel them, but could not move because of the restraints. The rest of my body was still numb. I was in so much pain I think death would have been better. I continued to push the button, but no one came. I was screaming and crying for a long time, and then finally, someone came through the door. The entire time I had been coming to this hospital, I never saw a black man or woman. I told him I was in pain and I needed some help. He said "I will try to get someone, but they hear you calling them. I am just the laundry man and happened to be walking by and heard you screaming from the hallway. I can't do nothing cause yall be in here screaming all the time, but I will let the nurse know. Hey son," he asked, "where yo folks?"

I looked up at him and wondered the same exact thing. The nurse finally came in after hours of me screaming and yelling and gave me some pain medicine, I guess telling the janitor helped. I couldn't tell whether it was day or night. Usually, I could see the street lights when they would open the windows. I heard someone outside of my room. It was real late at night. Maybe it was the janitor again because no one ever came in. I was hoping the nurse would come in soon because I could not sleep. The pain had started again and my lips were dry and so was my throat.

I laid in agony for a long time before a nurse came in. I knew there would be no sense in screaming because no one would come. She asked me how I was feeling. I told her I was in a lot of pain and that I was very thirsty. She was a new nurse. She was older and very nice. She said "I'm sorry I can't give you anything for pain until your doctor comes back, but I will give you some water". I said "thank you." I took one sip and it made me sick because I can feel the water going into my empty stomach. "I was not supposed to give you anything to eat or drink she said, but we will keep this to ourselves ok."

I nodded my head and asked her, "how long have I been here?"

"You have been in this room 3 days, but I would have to see how long you been in the hospital."

"Thanks," I said as she walked away. I finally rocked my own self to sleep from the constant pain.

The next day I can see the sun shining through my window. Some nurses and doctors came into the room asking me the same question, "how do you feel?" I told the doctor that was talking to me that I was in pain, thirsty and sore from the restraints. He said they had to restrain me for the surgery. The doctor said the surgery was very successful again. He said they had to fix my lens in the back of my eyes and they also found a small case of cataracts that they didn't see before. You will be able to see in a couple of days, he said. The other doctor butted in and said, "oh, you will also be able to eat solid foods tomorrow. I will give you something for pain, which will make you feel a whole lot better. You will be able to see very well," the Dr. stated, but as he said it, his colleagues looked at him with confused looks on their faces.

"How long have I been in here?" I asked.

"You have been in here for 3 weeks," he said. "You will probably go home next week. We just want to make sure your eyes are ok. In the meantime, we will try and contact your mother. Good luck," one of them said as they walked out of my room.

Chapter 7: Guinea Pig

I finally got my first real breakfast the next morning. They gave me some cereal, eggs, a piece of toast and juice. After the first couple of bites, I didn't want anymore. It made me feel bad, but after a couple of hours, I was ok and hungry again. By the time my food came for lunch, I was really ready to eat. I tried to finish because I could taste the food better, but I still only ate a few bites.

Later that night, the janitor came in my room and said hello. He said "I just wanted to come in and check on you and tell you I heard they are moving you to room 118 on the second floor because you are doing so much better. I am just glad to see you alert" he said, "because the other kids on this floor are barely moving and some of them are still groaning. I don't know what they do to those kids", he said, "because they are all bad off. Two kids have not come back to their rooms yet. It's been four days and no one has seen them. Anyway," he said, "I've said too much now. There are just a lot of rumors going around. I really wanted to tell you there are a lot of ladies upstairs in laundry praying for you and it looks like it has worked."

As he was leaving out, the same older nurse came in and moved my body. She said so I wouldn't get bed sores. "You look a lot better than you did yesterday. I didn't have to come in here at all. Last night survived. Don't pay any attention to me," she said, "I'm tired. I will bring you back some pain medicine and some pills for you to relax, doctors orders." She came back with the pills and some orange fluid for pain. She shut the door and I went to sleep, but I can only think about what she said about me surviving.

It seemed like more than a night had passed. I didn't know what day it was or what time it was. I still couldn't move and was very sore. I could only look straight ahead, couldn't look to the right or the left. I don't know how much time had passed before I saw anyone. Finally, a doctor came into the room. He was talking to one of the nurses. He came in and put his hands on my chest, arms and forehead. I could see him, but I couldn't feel his hands. They walked outside my room and talked. They didn't say anything to me. I stared at them talking until I dozed off again. When I woke up this time, I was in a different environment.

Chapter 8: Survivor

After all the medication they gave me was wearing off, I could hear clearer and I could move a little more than I could before. My chest felt like I had 400 lb weights on them. The left side of my body was heavy and was the hardest to move. My mouth was still terribly dry and I can hear a humming sound in my ear. I still had the tube in my nose and my sight was a little cloudy, but I guess everything was coming back, my vision and all of my senses.

Two nurses walked into the room, and one appeared to be crying. The other grabbed my chart from the foot of the bed, but she did not look at it. She was too busy trying to console the nurse who was crying. I didn't know what was going on, but it must have been very bad. Suddenly, a doctor and another nurse came running into my room moving the other nurses out of the way. They began to unhook all the tubes from my body. When they took the tube out my nose, it was like a breath of fresh air. I heard people scattering around in the hall and carts being pushed very fast. I heard one nurse scream "hurry, hurry." I saw another nurse crying. I wanted to ask what was going on. Everyone was going to the room next to me. The doctor was just standing in the hallway looking in a maze. I wish I knew what happened next door. I was trying to listen, then a nurse rushed into my room and said "you will be going home soon, and just ignore all the racket outside. We had a little emergency."

"Is the kid ok," I asked?

"You don't worry about next door," she said, "you just worry about getting out of here and not ever coming back. We called your mom, but we didn't get an answer. We will try again."

She asked how was I feeling. I told her my left side was heavy, humming in my head and ears, but my eyesight was clearing up.

"You will be ok," she said. "I will go call your mother again. You will be transferred to another location in the hospital. Someone who is not doing as well as you needs your bed. "Michael, she looked at me as she turned around to walk away, "you were very blessed because some of our other patients were not as…" then she stopped as if she was talking too much. "I will just call your mom," she said.

A couple hours passed and another nurse came in with a wheel chair.

She wanted me to get up on my own. It took forever to get into the wheelchair. It felt weird. I could see I was moving my legs and arms, but I barely felt them. A doctor came in and gave me a fluid to drink. He said it would make me feel better. The liquid made me cold again. It was cold going through my veins. Another Dr. came in and said "lets Go." He rolled me into the hallway. There were doctors and nurses everywhere. I saw plenty of sick black kids. Some were in wheelchairs and rolling carts moaning. I even saw the little girl from earlier. She was on a rolling cart right in front of me. She was looking towards me lying on her back with her head sideways staring me right in the face. She seemed as if she was paralyzed like I was. She couldn't move her body. I saw two other carts, but they had white sheets covering the bodies. I didn't understand what that meant until a later time. A doctor came by me and said get these carts and chairs out of this hallway and get someone up here from the morgue now." While I was waiting, I saw a clock and a calendar. It was Wednesday the 15th. I had been on this floor for 1 week because I came up here on the 7th. Someone, maybe a nurse or Doctor came from behind and started pushing me in the wheel chair. We got on the elevator and made a lot of twists and turns before we got to the waiting room.

There were a lot of old white people there. I was the only black and the youngest in the room. A nurse came behind me and asked me how I felt. I answered, "ok." She said I need you to try and walk for me Michael. I was afraid at first because my legs felt like jello, but surprisingly, I stood right up.

"Take your time," she said, "and go ahead and try and walk some more. Keep walking if you can." I walked around the waiting room. I didn't stumble or fall. I really felt good.

She said, "Ok champ. That's good enough." Another nurse came out and took my vital signs. She said "We finally got in touch with your mom. She should be here any minute now."

When I first got to the waiting room, it was full, but by the time mom got there, it was totally empty. I was the last patient in the waiting room. I saw mom come to the door and she looked very odd, I thought to myself. She came over to hug me when she saw me, but she was drunk and loud. This made me wonder if I was leaving hell for the fire.

Chapter 9: Homeward Bound

I'm home now and it seems like everything has gotten worse. The house was nasty with little or no food in the refrigerator and cabinets. Mom had started drinking more and more. She just gave up hope once my stepfather walked out and left her. She normally kept the house in order and clean. Months passed and mom was going on a downward spiral. She would cook pinto beans on Sunday and we would still be eating them on Wednesday. She would add water to them and add hot water cornbread to make a casserole out of them. Things got so bad that we used bacon grease for lotion, our scalps, and to shine our shoes. When we would go to the bus stop, the neighborhood kids would laugh because the dogs in the neighborhood would follow us because they smelled the bacon.

A couple of my uncles stopped by periodically - especially the one that didn't hold anything back. He said I looked different, but he was glad to see I made it ok.

One Sunday, my three sisters came over to my mom's house. I was very happy to see them. I had not seen them in years. They were very happy to see me too. After that one night, I never saw my sisters again. That's been 40 plus years.

I began to have some medical problems. My nose started back bleeding, unexpected dizziness, and bumps coming on my skin. Mom said she always wondered why my nose bled so bad. She thought the surgery would stop it. The bumps started appearing all over my body - my chest, arms, legs and hands were filled with them. They were small at first, but they started getting bigger and bigger. I always believed it had something to do with my surgery. I believed they fixed my eyes for a tradeoff of God knows what. I never told mom what happened in that hospital. I was always ashamed and afraid. The main reason I never told her is because I really did not want to know the real truth, and that is that my mother allowed all of this to happen. My mother asked me if I met the little boy down the street because he passed away. She said she didn't know why. All she knew was that he was on the same floor as I was - in the room next to me. Oh my God, I thought, that's why everyone was rushing that day. Then, I remembered the shoes under that white sheet.

Chapter 10: Aftermath

When I was sixteen, those little bumps still covered my body. They grew very slowly, and my nose was still prone to bleeding. I was also dizzy a lot, but I became used to it.

My sexual peak was kicking in and, when I was with girls my age, they were terrified and scared because I was so big. When word got around, I was called Horse Dick. I was very embarrassed at first, but that was when the older women started coming into the picture. Before I knew it, I was sleeping with the lady next door. She was twenty-six. I also slept with my uncle's girlfriend; she was twenty-four. Another neighbor I was thirty. Later, I dated a lady who worked in my leasing office for three years. She was thirty- two at the time. She taught me a lot, especially where oral sex was concerned. She said, because I was so big, I had to get a woman wet before penetrating.

After our painful breakup, I matured a lot. I used her tips and philosophy on girls my age. It worked sometimes. I learned to have oral sex in the dark so I could sneak myself in before the girl knew how big I was. I must say that I did have a lot of fun. I even had quite a few marriage proposals, but, because I was still dealing with the sadness of my childhood, I never took any of them up on their offers. I was confused and had little or no guidance in life as far as relationships were concerned. The women that I was seriously involved with were all about sex, sex, sex. I enjoyed it, but I was looking for more. It was one behind another. It was married women when I attended college. It was instructors a couple of times, too. When I was working on a job, it was my boss. The list goes on and on.

In the early 80s, I was in a threesome for nearly two years. It was just us three. They were two very attractive women. We did everything together, and it wasn't just about the sex. We really enjoyed each other. My dumb ass called it off. That one decision has haunted me. That was probably the only time I was happy - not because of the sex, but because of the chemistry the three of us shared. We all respected each other and cared about each other. It was fun, but I was looking for a one-on-one relationship.

Chapter 11: Growing Up

I am now in my fifties. A lot has happened and a lot has come and gone. The ghost of my past still lingers with me. I still jump up in a cold sweat from nightmares. The bumps or whatever they are still grow and form their own textures. They stretch from my chest to my back to my arms. They are over my entire body. Sometimes, when I look at myself in the mirror, I feel like a freak. The bumps are now causing me pain. I attended a local Doctor's office recently and she told me these were not keloids and she had no idea what they are. She said she has never seen anything like them. She says it looks like a chemical reaction that's causing my skin to puff outwards. They cause me a lot of pain and now they are bleeding. New ones will pop up. The doctor did multiple tests. She found nothing. She said I am very fit and healthy for a man in his fifties. The doctors only came up with I have extremely high white blood cell count, but everything is normal. They only can speculate, but I see the way they look at me. I take pain pills for pain as needed. My doctor has sent me to all kinds of specialists and all have that same stupid looks on their faces - like what did I do? I want to yell and say I was a damn Lab monkey.

I now have a better understanding. Looking back at my past, yes I did need surgery on my eyes, but it was a trade off for me to be their experiment. They used poor little black kids in the 60s for guinea pigs and lab monkeys. I believe the government gave them a facility to do experiments on poor black children.

My mother did not have any money or health insurance, but I was given a very expensive surgery. Yea right, nothing in life is free. I saw so many children die at that hospital, but I was too young to understand what was going on. The memories of the kids covered with those white sheets still haunt me.

My mother has passed now, and I still don't understand why she did some of the things she did, but I always loved her still. My mom had a hard life. She had to raise her siblings after her mom was killed. She was really given a bad hand in life. Mom had 11 children in all: Dwayne, Penny, Linda, Terry, Lyn, Joe, Ray, Jimmie, Shelia, Paula and myself. Those she didn't give away, died. I guess I was meant to survive. I remember my sister Shelia. She was going back and forth to the hospital just like I did, but one day she never came home and mama never talked about it. We never asked what happen to my sister Shelia.

I had not started going to the hospital yet, but I sure remember her doing the exact thing I was doing, and she could see perfectly clear. I once heard mama tell someone she was around 25, and she passed in the hospital. My younger sister is Paula, whom I love very much to this day. My older sister Penny, is the one I've seen more recently. It has been 30 years since I have seen her. I saw her at a bus stop. We talked and she invited me over to her house. I took her home and we were sitting down reminiscing when her boyfriend came in and started cursing at her and she asked me to leave. She had told me he was abusing her. Wow, she was just like mom. I never saw her again and she never called - although that day I gave her my number.

I have no regrets in my life now. I am very successful. I have my own home, a very good job and solely dependent on myself. I have three children of my own - two sons and a daughter that I love very much..

Chapter 12: Dealing With My Past

I have often looked back on my life and all the experiments that were done to me and one thing I'm proud of is that I didn't let my circumstances or blows life through at me make me fall. I deal with it and I fight the demons of my past daily, but by writing this book, people will get to know what happen to all the missing little black children in the 50s and 60s.

Chapter 13: Final Thought

I know to some people, this story may seem as if it's fiction, but I can really tell you that I have woken up many mornings with unexplainable pain in my chest and just wished on so many nights that this was all just a bad dream. I have to live with this pain every day – looking at my body and the lesions all over it – not ever being able to war a sleeveless shirt in public, constantly wondering why it was me who chosen out of all my mother's kids. Why did I have to be the chosen one?

I still don't know til this day, what happened to my sister Sheila. I often wonder if she suffered much, or if she was one of the ones who moaned and groaned until she was eventually put to rest – covered with the infamous white sheet. I asked my mom after my incident where Sheila had been and if she went through the same thing I did. She would just tell me not to worry about Sheila. She was in a better place. She never gave me a straight answer. The think that I remember most about Shelia is that she was beautiful and that she did not want to go to that hospital the last time. I remember her kicking and screaming as my mom and stepdad threw her in the car. Now, 40 plus years later, I still hear those screeching cries and screams of her saying "no, no, no!" At the time, I didn't understand why she didn't want to go. Of course, I soon found out on my own.

Another mystery was the pretty little girl who was age on the stretcher in the hallway. Her eyes stared down at me. This had to be the first time I could see crystal clear. She had a look on her face that was begging me to help her, but she could not speak. There was this look of desperation on her face. It was as if she was saying "If you don't help me, I will never see you again." I felt as helpless as she. I wished I could have become one of those super heroes I read about in comic books right then. I wanted to grab her and fly away. But I am not a super hero so I all I could do was stare back into her helpless eyes as they pushed me away. As it turned out, I never did see her again.

There are so many unanswered questions I have for my mom, the doctors, and my family, but every time I inquired, no one seemed to have any answers. I truly believe this is what drove my mother to drinking. She went from being the best mother in the world to the worse woman I didn't know. She was almost nonresponsive to life itself. She woke up and went to bed in the same clothes daily. She became promiscuous, but so lonely at the same time. There are a lot of questions I still have, but I know now that none of them will ever be answered. I still live with those mysteries every day. I'm still haunted by the painful memories of that small county hospital in a quaint little town in Mississippi. Little black kids went there, but some never came back. They just became part of the missing children of the south.

According to the National Center for Missing & Exploited Children, more than 2,000 children are reported missing in the United States each day. 146, 000 Black children are reported missing each year – and often with little to no media coverage. According to Nicole Wilson, co-founder of the Black and Missing Foundation Inc., a lot of the blame is the bias reporting in the newsroom. When Jon Benet Ramsey was stolen from her room, it received National coverage and we heard about it for days. On the other hand, when teenager Phylicia Barnes was reported missing in North Carolina, we never knew who she was until she was found dead months later in Maryland. Her death got one day of news coverage – that's all.

Blacks need to speak up and demand coverage from the media. They need to be more involved and more on watch for the missing and exploited children in and from our community. It has been said that these children are not news worthy or not worthy at all because most of them are poor. I say, they may be poor, but they are still someone's son, daughter, brother, or sister….they could have been you. I'm one of the lucky ones. I survived being a lab monkey. So many others were not so lucky. This is my story. What is yours?

Lab Monkey: I Survived
... a true story...

Resources for Missing & Exploited Children

Missing-Child Clearinghouse Program

[source:http://www.missingkids.com/missingkids/servlet/
ServiceServlet?LanguageCountry=en_US&PageId=1421]

Each of the 50 states, plus the District of Columbia, Puerto Rico, U.S. Virgin Islands, Canada, and the Netherlands, provides resources for missing children, their families, and the professionals who serve them. These resources are referred to as missing-child clearinghouses.

The missing-child clearinghouses primarily focus on networking, information dissemination, training development and delivery, data collection, and provision of technical assistance in cases of missing and sexually exploited children.

Here is a list of missing-child clearinghouses in each of those jurisdictions.

ALABAMA
Alabama Bureau of Investigation/Missing Children
P.O. Box 1511
Montgomery, AL 36102-1511
(800) 228-7688
FAX: (334) 353-2563
www.dps.state.al.us/abi

ALASKA
Alaska State Troopers
Missing Persons Clearinghouse
3925 Tudor Centre Road
Anchorage, AK 99508
(907) 269-5058 / (800) 478-9333 (in-state only)
FAX: (907) 269-0732

ARIZONA
Arizona Department of Public Safety Criminal Investigations Research
Unit P.O. Box 6638
Phoenix, AZ 85005 (602) 644-5868
FAX: (602) 644-8709

ARKANSAS
Office of Attorney General
Missing Children Services Program
323 Center Street, Ste. 200
Little Rock, AR 72201
(501) 682-1020 / (800) 448-3014 (in-state only)
FAX: (501) 682-6704
www.ag.state.ar.us

CALIFORNIA
California Department of Justice Missing/Unidentified Persons Unit P.
O. Box 903387
Sacramento, CA 94203-3870 (916) 227-3290 / (800) 222-3463
FAX: (916) 227-3270 http://ag.ca.gov/missing

COLORADO
Colorado Bureau of Investigation
Missing Person/Children Unit
710 Kipling Street, Suite 200
Denver, CO 80215
(303) 239-4251
FAX: (303) 239-5788

CONNECTICUT
Connecticut State Police Missing Persons
P.O. Box 2794
Middletown, CT 06457-9294
(860) 685-8190 / (800) 367-5678 (in-state only)
Emergency Messaging: (860) 685-8190
FAX: (860) 685-8346.

DELAWARE
Delaware State Police
State Bureau of Identification
1407 N. DuPont Hwy.
Dover, DE 19903
(302) 739-5883
FAX: (302) 739-5888

DISTRICT OF COLUMBIA D.C.
Metropolitan Police Dept. Missing Persons/Youth Division
1700 Rhode Island Avenue, N.E.
Washington, DC 20018
(202) 576-6768
FAX: (202) 576-6561

FLORIDA
Florida Department of Law Enforcement Missing Children Information
Clearinghouse P.O. Box 1489
Tallahassee, FL 32302
(850) 410-8585 / (888) 356-4774 (nationwide)
FAX: (850) 410-8599
www.fdle.state.fl.us

GEORGIA
Georgia Bureau of Investigation
GISAC
P.O. Box 29649
Atlanta, GA 30359

(404) 486-6420
(800) 282-6564 (nationwide)
FAX: (404) 486-6446

HAWAII
Missing Child Center - Hawaii
Department of the Attorney General
235 S. Beretania Street, Suite 401
425 Queen Street
Honolulu, HI 96813
(808) 586-1449
Hotline: (808) 753-9797
FAX: (808) 586-1097
www.missingchildcenterhawaii.com

IDAHO
Idaho Bureau of Criminal Identification
Missing Persons Clearinghouse
P.O. Box 700
Meridian, ID 83680-0700
(208) 884-7154 / (888) 777-3922 (nationwide)
FAX: (208) 884-7193
www.isp.state.id.us

ILLINOIS
Illinois State Police
Clearinghouse for Missing Persons
2200 S. Dirksen Parkway, Suite 238
Springfield, Illinois 62703-4528
(217) 785-4341 / 1-800-843-5763 (Nationwide)
FAX 217-557-0565

INDIANA
Indiana State Police
Indiana Missing Children Clearinghouse
100 North Senate Avenue

Third Floor
Indianapolis, IN 46204-2259
(317) 232-8310 / (800) 831-8953 (nationwide)
FAX: (317) 233-3057
www.state.in.us/isp

IOWA

Missing Person Information Clearinghouse
Division of Criminal Investigation
215 E. 7th Street
Des Moines, IA 50319
(515) 725-6036 / (800) 346-5507 (nationwide)
FAX: (515) 725-6035
www.iowaonline.state.ia.us/mpic/

KANSAS

Kansas Bureau of Investigation
Missing/Unidentified Person Clearinghouse
1620 S.W. Tyler Street
Topeka, KS 66604
(785) 296-8200
FAX: (785) 296-6781
www.accesskansas.org/kbi/

KENTUCKY

Kentucky Intelligence & Information Fusion Center
200 Mero Street, Suite 127
Frankfort, KY 40601
(502) 564-1020 / (800) KIDS-SAF (543-7723) - nationwide
FAX: (502) 564-5315

LOUISIANA

Louisiana State Police
Louisiana Clearinghouse for Missing & Exploited Children
7919 Independence Blvd. A-2
Baton Rouge, LA 70806

1-800-434-8007
Fax: (225) 925-4766
http://lsp.org/cid.html

MAINE
Maine State Police - Missing Children Clearinghouse
CID 1
1 Game Farm Road
Gray, ME 04039
(207) 657-5710
FAX: (207) 657-5748

MARYLAND
Maryland Center for Missing Children
Maryland State Police
1201 Reisterstown Road
Baltimore, MD 21208
(410) 290-1620 / (800) 637-5437 (nationwide)
FAX: (410) 290-1831

MASSACHUSETTS
Massachusetts State Police
Commonwealth Fusion Center
124 Acton Street
Maynard, MA 01754 (978) 451-3700
FAX: (978) 451-3707

MICHIGAN
Michigan State Police
Michigan Intelligence Operations Center
Michigan State Police
714 South Harrison Road
East Lansing, MI 48823 (517) 241-7183
FAX: (517) 241-6815

MINNESOTA
Minnesota State Clearinghouse
MN Bureau of Criminal Apprehension
1430 Maryland Avenue E.
St. Paul, MN 55106
(651) 793-7000 (24/7)
FAX: (651) 793-7015

MISSISSIPPI
Mississippi Highway Patrol
Criminal Information Center
3891 Highway 468 West
Pearl, MS 39208
(601) 933-2656
FAX: (601) 933-2677

MISSOURI
Missouri State Highway Patrol
Missing Persons Unit
P. O. Box 568
Jefferson City, MO 65102
(573) 526-6178 / (800) 877-3452 (nationwide)
FAX: (573) 526-5577

MONTANA
Montana Department of Justice Missing/Unidentified Persons P.O. Box
201402
303 N. Roberts Street, Room 471
Helena, MT 59620-1402
(406) 444-2800
FAX: (406) 444-4453

NEBRASKA
Nebraska State Patrol
CID/Missing Persons Clearinghouse
P. O. Box 94907

Lincoln, NE 68509-4907
(402) 479-4986 / 1-877-441-5678 (toll free)
FAX: (402) 479-4054

NEVADA
Nevada State Advocate for Missing and Exploited Children
Office of the Attorney General
555 E. Washington Ave., Suite 3900
Las Vegas, NV 89101-6208
(702) 486-3539
(800) 992-0900 (in-state only)
FAX: (702) 486-2377

NEW HAMPSHIRE
New Hampshire State Police Investigative Services Bureau Major Crime
Unit
91 Airport Rd
Concord, NH 03301
(603) 271-2663 / (800) 852-3411 (in-state only)
24-hour referral number (603) 271-3636
FAX: (603) 271-2520

NEW JERSEY
New Jersey State Police
Missing Persons Unit
P. O. Box 7068
W. Trenton, NJ 08628
(609) 882-2000 (see extensions) / (800) 709-7090 (nationwide)
FAX: (609) 882-2719
http://www.njsp.org/divorg/invest/mpce-unit.html

NEW MEXICO
New Mexico Department of Public Safety
ATTN: Law Enforcement Records
P. O. Box 1628

Santa Fe, NM 87504-1628
(800) 457-3463
FAX: (505) 827-3399

NEW YORK
New York Division of Criminal Justice Services
Missing Persons Clearinghouse
4 Tower Place
Albany, NY 12203
(800) 346-3543 (nationwide)
FAX: (518) 457-6965
http://criminaljustice.state.ny.us

NORTH CAROLINA
North Carolina Center for Missing Persons
4706 Mail Service Center
Raleigh, NC 27699-4706
(800) 522-5437 (nationwide)
FAX: (919) 715-1682

NORTH DAKOTA
North Dakota Clearinghouse for Missing Children
North Dakota Bureau of Criminal Investigation
4205 N. State Street
Bismarck, ND 58503
(701) 328-8171
FAX: (701) 328-5510

OHIO
Missing Persons Unit
Ohio Attorney General's Office
Criminal Justice Initiatives
150 Gay Street, 25th Floor
Columbus, OH 43215-4231 (614) 466-5610
(800) 325-5604 (nationwide)
www.mcc.ag.state.oh.us/

OKLAHOMA
Missing Person Clearinghouse Oklahoma State Bureau of Investigation
Criminal Intelligence Office
6600 N. Harvey
Oklahoma City, OK 73116
(405) 879-2645 / (800) 522-8017
FAX: (405) 879-2967

OREGON
Oregon State Police
Missing Children Clearinghouse
255 Capital Street, NE, 4th Floor
Salem, OR 97310
(503) 934-0188 / (800) 282-7155 (in-state only)
FAX: (503) 363-5475
www.osp.state.or.us

PENNSYLVANIA
Pennsylvania State Police Missing Persons Unit
Bureau of Criminal Investigation
1800 Elmerton Avenue
Harrisburg, PA 17110
(717) 346-3378
FAX: (717) 705-2306

RHODE ISLAND
Rhode Island State Police
Missing & Exploited Children Unit
311 Danielson Pike
North Scituate, RI 02857
(401) 444-1125
FAX: (401) 444-1149

SOUTH CAROLINA
South Carolina Law Enforcement Division
Missing Person Information Center

P. O. Box 21398
Columbia, SC 29221-1398
(803) 737-9000 / (800) 322-4453 (nationwide)
FAX: (803) 896-7595

SOUTH DAKOTA
South Dakota Attorney General's Office
Division of Criminal Investigation
1302 East Highway 14, Suite 5
Pierre, SD 57501-8505
(605) 773-3331
FAX: (605) 773-4629

TENNESSEE
Tennessee Bureau of Investigation
Criminal Intelligence Unit
901 R.S. Gass Blvd.
Nashville, TN 37206
(615) 744-4000
FAX: (615) 744-4655

TEXAS
Texas Department of Public Safety Criminal Intelligence Service Missing
Persons Clearinghouse P.O. Box 4087
Austin, TX 78773-0422 (512) 424-5074
(800) 346-3243 (in-state only) FAX: (512) 424?2885 www.txdps.state.
tx.us/mpch

UTAH
Utah Department of Public Safety Bureau of Criminal Identification Utah
Missing Persons Clearinghouse
3888 West 5400 South
P.O. Box 148280
Salt Lake City, UT 84114-8280
(801)965-4686 / (888) 770-6477 (nationwide) FAX: (801) 965-4749

VERMONT
Vermont State Police
103 South Main Street
Waterbury, VT 05671
(802) 244-8727
FAX: (802) 241-5552

VIRGINIA
Virginia State Police Department Missing Children's Clearinghouse P. O.
Box 27472
Richmond, VA 23261
(804) 674-2026 / (800) 822-4453 (800 VACHILD)
FAX: (804) 674-2105

WASHINGTON
Washington State Patrol Missing persons Unit
P. O. Box 2347
Olympia, WA 98507-2347
(800) 543-5678 (nationwide)
FAX: (360) 704-2971

WEST VIRGINIA
West Virginia State Police
Missing Children Clearinghouse
725 Jefferson Road
South Charleston, WV 25309-1698
(304) 558-1467 / (800) 352-0927 (nationwide)
FAX: (304) 558-1470

WISCONSIN
Wisconsin Missing and Exploited Children
Wisconsin AMBER Alert Coordinator
P. O. Box 7857
Madison, WI 53701-2718
(608) 266-1671 / (800) THE-HOPE (in-state only)
FAX: (608) 267-2777

WYOMING
Wyoming Office of the Attorney General
Division of Criminal Investigation
316 West 22nd
Cheyenne, WY 82002
(307) 777-7537
Control Terminal: (307) 777-7545
FAX: (307) 777-8900

CANADA
National Missing Children's Services
1200 Vanier Parkway
Ottawa, Ontario, CN K1A OR2
(613) 993-1525 / (877) 318-3576 (Toll Free)
After Hours Urgent Calls (pager): (613) 760-6689
FAX: (613) 993-5430
http://www.ourmissingchildren.gc.ca

PUERTO RICO
Missing Children Program
Centro Estatal Para Niños Desparecidos y Victimas de Abuso
P.O. Box 9023899
Old San Juan, Puerto Rico 00902-3899
(787) 729-2068 / 2457
(800) 995-NINO - limited calling area
FAX: (787) 722-0809

U.S. VIRGIN ISLANDS
U.S. Virgin Islands Police Department Patrick Sweeney Police Headquarters
RR02 Kingshill
St. Croix, VI 00850 (340) 772-2211
Fax: (340) 772-2626

NETHERLANDS POLICE
Dutch National Police
P.O. Box 3016
2700 KX Zoetermeer
The Netherlands
011-31-79-345-9748
FAX: 011-31-79-345-8881
http://nl.missingkids.com

After having gone through my ordeal being a lab monkey, I found out later that there were lots of other medical experiments done on the poor, minorities, prisoners, orphans and others who either didn't have control of their situations or the knowledge of what was being done to them. Here is a list of other medical experiments I found that were conducted in the U.S. long before my situation and long after:

(1845 - 1849)
JMarion Sims, later hailed as the "father of gynecology," performs <u>medical experiments</u> on enslaved African women without <u>anesthesia</u>. These women would usually die of <u>infection</u> soon after surgery. Based on his belief that the movement of newborns' skull <u>bones</u> during protracted births <u>causes</u> trismus, he also uses a shoemaker's awl, a pointed tool shoemakers use to make holes in leather, to practice moving the skull bones of <u>babies</u> born to enslaved mothers (<u>Brinker</u>).

(1895)
<u>New York</u> pediatrician Henry Heiman infects a 4-year-old boy whom he calls "an idiot with chronic epilepsy" with gonorrhea as part of a medical experiment (<u>"Human Experimentation: Before the Nazi Era</u> <u>and After"</u>).

(1896)
Dr. Arthur Wentworth turns 29 <u>children</u> at Boston's Children's Hospital into human <u>guinea pigs</u> when he performs spinal taps on them, just to test whether the procedure is harmful (<u>Sharav</u>).

(1906)
Harvard professor Dr. Richard Strong infects <u>prisoners</u> in the Philippines with cholera to study the <u>disease</u>; 13 of them die. He compensates survivors with cigars and cigarettes. During the Nuremberg Trials, Nazi <u>doctors</u> cite this study to justify their own medical experiments (<u>Greger</u>, <u>Sharav</u>).

(1911)
Dr. Hideyo Noguchi of the Rockefeller Institute for Medical Research publishes data on injecting an inactive syphilis preparation into the skin of 146 <u>hospital</u> patients and normal children in an attempt to develop a

skin test for syphilis. Later, in 1913, several of these children's parents sue Dr. Noguchi for allegedly infecting their children with syphilis ("Reviews and Notes: History of Medicine: Subjected to Science: Human Experimentation in America before the Second World War").

(1913)

Medical experimenters "test" 15 children at the children's home St. Vincent's House in Philadelphia with tuberculin, resulting in permanent blindness in some of the children. Though the Pennsylvania House of Representatives records the incident, the researchers are not punished for the experiments ("Human Experimentation: Before the Nazi Era and After").

(1915)

Dr. Joseph Goldberger, under order of the U.S. Public Health Office, produces Pellagra, a debilitating disease that affects the central nervous system, in 12 Mississippi inmates to try to find a cure for the disease. One test subject later says that he had been through "a thousand hells." In 1935, after millions die from the disease, the director of the U.S Public Health Office would finally admit that officials had known that it was caused by a niacin deficiency for some time, but did nothing about it because it mostly affected poor African- Americans. During the Nuremberg Trials, Nazi doctors used this study to try to justify their medical experiments on concentration camp inmates (Greger; Cockburn and St. Clair, eds.).

Lab Monkey: I Survived
... a true story...

About the Author

Michael Young now resides happily in Atlanta, GA. He works full time and lives a normal single life. He has three adult children, all of whom he holds dear to his heart, and a host of friends and colleagues. In his free time, he still reflects on the pains of his childhood, but looks forward with both hope for even better days ahead and gratitude for having made it this far in one piece.

Printed in the United States
By Bookmasters